The Library of
HOLIDAYS™

Flag Day

Leslie C. Kaplan

The Rosen Publishing Group's
PowerKids Press™
New York

To Dad

Published in 2004 by The Rosen Publishing Group, Inc.
29 East 21st Street, New York, NY 10010

First Edition

Editor: Jannell Khu

Book Design: Michael J. Caroleo and Michael de Guzman

Photo Credits: Cover © CORBIS; p. 4 © Mike Powell/Getty Images; p. 7 courtesy of National Flag Day Americanism Center and (inset) courtesy of National Flag Day Americanism Center/Ozaukee County Historical Society; p. 8 © Mimmo Jodice/CORBIS; p. 11 (foreground) © Rosen; pp. 11 (background), 15 © EyeWire; p 12 © SuperStock; pp. 16, 20 © Bettmann/CORBIS; p. 19 © Steve Chenn/CORBIS; p. 22 © Joseph Sohm; ChromoSohm Inc./CORBIS.

Kaplan, Leslie C.
Flag Day / Leslie C. Kaplan.
     p. cm. — (The library of holidays)
Includes bibliographical references and index.
ISBN 0-8239-6659-3 (library binding)
1. Flag Day—Juvenile literature. [1. Flag Day. 2. Holidays.] I. Title. II. Series.
JK1761 .K36 2004
394.263—dc21

                                                                 2002007621

Manufactured in the United States of America

Contents

What Is Flag Day?

Americans celebrate Flag Day on June 14. This date marks the birthday of the American flag, which was **officially** adopted by **Congress** on June 14, 1777. On Flag Day, Americans fly the red-white-and-blue flag beside buildings and homes. Students take part in flag-raising **ceremonies**. Communities throughout America gather for speeches and parades to honor this important **symbol** of their country. The flag is a reminder of all the great ideals for which many Americans have fought and died.

The American flag stands for freedom, equality, justice, and hope.

How Flag Day Began

On June 14, 1885, a Wisconsin teacher named Bernard J. Cigrand celebrated the flag's birthday with his students. He later wrote newspaper articles and made public speeches asking Americans to adopt June 14 as Flag Day officially. Cigrand's efforts renewed America's interest in the flag. **Patriotic** groups in Pennsylvania, New York, and Illinois pushed to start a national celebration of the flag's birthday. Finally in 1949, President Harry S. Truman signed a law that established June 14 as Flag Day in America.

The upper right photo is of Bernard J. Cigrand, and the building is Stoney Hill School, where he was a teacher. ▶

Flags in Earlier Times

People have used flags for thousands of years. Early flags were not made of cloth. It is believed that ancient Egyptians made the first flags about 5,000 years ago. They made flags out of feathers, which were symbols of their rulers. Some of the world's earliest flags were animal skins attached to wooden poles. The Chinese may have been the first to sew cloth flags. Although flags can be made of different materials, their chief importance lies in that for which the flags stand.

◀ *People have used flags for centuries. The man on this stone painting, which is hundreds of years old, carries a flag.*

A New Flag Is Needed

Although the American **colonies** were under British rule from 1607 to 1776, they wanted their own flag. They made a new flag with a copy of Britain's flag in the corner. This flag was used during the **American Revolution** when George Washington took command of the American army. He raised the flag near his base in Massachusetts. The flag confused the British soldiers. They mistakenly thought that Washington wanted to give up when they saw the British flag in the corner of the raised flag. Clearly a new flag was needed!

The colonists made a flag with 7 red stripes and 6 white stripes. They placed Britain's flag in the top left corner. ▶

Who Made the New Flag?

A popular story has it that in 1776, George Washington visited a seamstress named Betsy Ross. Upon Washington's request, Ross made a new American flag. Although there is no proof of this, Ross's **descendants** have signed **affidavits** to say this story is true. Some people believe that Francis Hopkinson of New Jersey is the one who made the flag. In 1780, Hopkinson presented a bill to Congress for this service, but he was never paid. Others think that he designed the flag and that Ross sewed it.

Some people believe that Betsy Ross gave George Washington the idea to have five-pointed stars in the American flag.

13

The Look of the Flag

The first American flag had 13 stripes and 13 stars to represent the 13 original American colonies. The flag's 13 white stars appeared in a blue box in the flag's top left corner. By 1795, Vermont and Kentucky had joined the United States. Congress added two more stars and two more stripes. The flag was getting crowded! In 1818, Congress passed a law stating that the American flag would always have 13 stripes. However, for each new state, a star would be added. As America continued to grow, new stars were added.

Today's flag has 50 stars to represent each state in America. Alaska and Hawaii are the newest states. They joined in 1959. ▶

"The Star-Spangled Banner"

The American flag is the only flag in the world with a national **anthem** written about it. This song is "The Star-Spangled Banner." During the War of 1812, Francis Scott Key wrote the words to it in the poem "The Defense of Fort McHenry." The United States was at war against Britain and Key watched the British bomb Fort McHenry in Maryland. The next morning, the American flag still flew over the fort! This meant that the British had not won. Later, Key's poem was set to music and was renamed "The Star-Spangled Banner."

◄ *Key watched from a ship as the British bombed Fort McHenry. He wrote "The Defense of Fort McHenry" in September 1814.*

The Pledge of Allegiance

Francis Bellamy was a church minister who became famous for something he wrote. In 1892, Bellamy wrote special words for Americans to say while looking at their flag. What Bellamy wrote became known as the Pledge of Allegiance. Allegiance means loyalty to a nation or a cause. A pledge is a promise. Congress made Bellamy's pledge an official promise of loyalty to the United States in 1942. Nobody is required to say the Pledge of Allegiance. The right not to say the pledge is protected by the **First Amendment**.

Many schoolchildren all over America face the American flag in the morning and say the Pledge of Allegiance. ▶

Where the Flags Are

Throughout America, the American flag is a familiar sight. People pin tiny flags on their clothes and attach flag stickers to their cars. They wave flags during parades on Flag Day and on Independence Day. The American flag is also flown outside the country. It flies above U.S. **embassies** in countries around the world. Wherever Americans have explored, the flag has gone with them. It has been planted at the North and South Poles and stands on the highest mountains. The American flag has even been carried to the Moon!

◄ *In 1969, astronaut Edwin E. Aldrin Jr. stood beside an American flag on the Moon. It was placed there during the* Apollo 11 *mission.*

Celebrating Flag Day

There are many ways to celebrate Flag Day. You can honor the flag's birthday by saying the Pledge of Allegiance and by singing "The Star-Spangled Banner." Join others in a flag-raising ceremony. Learn how to treat the flag properly. Displaying the flag with respect is a way to honor it. The flag should fly outdoors from sunrise to sunset only. It should never touch the ground. During bad weather, the flag should stay inside. The flag should be treated with respect, because it is an important symbol of America.

Glossary

affidavits (a-fih-DAY-vihts) Written, sworn statements of truth.

American Revolution (uh-MER-uh-ken reh-vuh-LOO-shun) Battles that soldiers from the colonies fought against Britain for freedom, from 1775 to 1783.

anthem (AN-thum) A sacred song or hymn.

ceremonies (SER-ih-moh-neez) Special series of acts done on certain occasions.

colonies (KAH-luh-neez) Large groups of people who have left their own country to live in a new land but who are still ruled by the leaders and the laws of their old country.

Congress (KON-gres) The part of the U.S. government that makes laws.

descendants (dih-SEN-dents) People born of a certain family or group.

embassies (EM-buh-seez) Official homes and offices in a foreign country.

First Amendment (FURST uh-MEND-ment) A change to the Constitution, or central law, of the United States, which secures the right to free expression.

officially (uh-FIH-shul-lee) Having proof that something is formal or legal.

patriotic (pay-tree-AH-tik) Showing one's love for one's country.

symbol (SIM-bul) An object or a design that stands for something else.

Index

Web Sites

Due to the changing nature of Internet links, PowerKids Press has developed an online list of Web sites related to the subject of this book. This site is updated regularly. Please use this link to access the list: www.powerkidslinks.com/LHOL/flag